HEADLONG

UNIVERSITY OF UTAH PRESS POETRY SERIES

JAMES McKEAN

HEADLONG

University of Utah Press   Salt Lake City   1987

UNIVERSITY OF UTAH PRESS POETRY SERIES
DAVE SMITH, EDITOR

See Acknowledgments, page 68, for permission statements.
∞ The paper in this book meets the standards for permanence
and durability established by the Committee on Production Guidelines
for Book Longevity of the Council on Library Resources.

LIBRARY OF CONGRESS CATALOGING-IN-PUBLICATION DATA

McKean, James, 1946 Jul. 4–
    Headlong.
    ✓ (University of Utah Press poetry series)
    I. Title. II. Series.
PS3563.C3737H4   1987   811'.54   86-28200
ISBN 0-87480-273-3

for my family

THE GIFT

Beneath an incomplete set
of *World Book Encyclopedia*
and two movie magazines
in the corner of Gracie's Junk Store,
Dillon, Montana,
I found
Mrs. Ruth S. Julian's
1898 edition of
*A Selection from the
Discourses of Epictetus*
in which she had pressed
one hundred and twenty-seven
four leaf clovers.

CONTENTS

I

GREEN LAKE

What I remember most
is my mother's hand
squeezing my arm as if
she thought I was going
to fly and my father,
his hat off, in the water
for the first time
I could tell, hand in hand
with other men. They
walked back and forth,
and the red buoys waved
like the roses at home
in the wind. Not much more:
women, their children
wrapped in towels, and
when we left, my father
saying, "Something will
turn up. It always does."
Then my mother silent,
her face a ghost
in the window of the car,
and for days afterward
the shape of her hand,
bigger than mine,
rising slowly to the surface
of my skin.

LEARNING TO READ

My father belongs outside,
measuring the rock wall behind our house
or digging in the ground
for the right stone.

He does not want my help,
I think, turning a page in a book
that hides all the answers. I try
the words beneath my breath,

remembering how he once held a flashcard up
and the letters went white
with my staring.
One more word. Say it, he'd said,

pointing to the chair
he would not lean into,
to the doilies, their pins
catching his sleeve. I followed his hand

like a flushed bird
past the hearth, the curtains pulled tight
against the sun, until at last . . .
reading was up to me.

I change the letters in my book
to the tracks of a gull,
chase it off the page out the window,
the gull going blue and noisy.

A jay! Down from its nest,
past my father's lifting stones,
his turning them over and over
the puzzle he is making.

The stones fit. I wonder if places
are there to begin with.
I watch him step back, speak to no one
but himself, as sure as I am

his wall holds the house up
and the stones will stay put,
tamped into place by his whispers
like my word for home, *home*.

AFTER LISTENING TO JACK TEAGARDEN . . .

I will blame him,
the man who convinced my mother
there was talent in long arms,
whose baton held me lock-stepped
all summer in three songs,
who never revealed the old name
for trombone is sackbut,
as awkward as the black vinyl case
I banged against my knees
in a neighborhood where salvation
meant running. *Sackbut*,
the first girl I ever kissed,
wet-mouthed and blowing
and not a sound, much less a sob
of music. I blame him
for one lost summer, my mouth full of oil,
stuck spit valves, the slide
dented over and over by the ground.
Yes, him, for my bird-flushing,
window-rattling squawks,
for the anonymous gift of a mute,
for my memory of him yet
like the music stand I could never fold
right again. May he hear me
once more in the Lake City parade,
timed by his whistle,
all oxfords and a new white shirt.
May he forgive my faking
the two songs I never learned.
May he accept the blame
for my marching out of step up the rear
of the Ridgecrest Mounted Posse,
their horses farting
as I lost myself in "Sweet Georgia Brown,"
the only song I remembered
as loud as I could.

ROWING FOR WATER

Pushing off, I set the oar blades
flat against the cove and pull too hard.
Before me my father leans on his shovel,
and my mother kneels, scooping butter clams
from the sand. They do not look up
at my first rowing for water,
the sun hot on my back, and the oars,
hardly locked, banging my shins
as I zigzag through the heavy, green Sound.
I don't remember its looking this hard
when my father cut a narrow wake
from the shore, the tips of his oars spinning
whirlpools like the silver filigree
of my mother's Norwegian jewelry,
smaller and smaller until he disappeared
into the steep bank across the cove
where the catch barrels sit moss-covered
and hidden. Now I back into everything.
The smoke I've lined up on drifts away.
My hands blister, the skiff yaws
in the wind, and my haste moves nothing
except the jerricans clanking in the stern.
I have never lifted them full before
as my father has, hobbling up the beach,
five gallons of water in each hand
for my mother and me, who always drink first.
But the last time, I asked what took him so long,
and he drank before me, taking a long time,
with a look on his face as if he had never tasted
anything so good.

LA PUSH

Hiding beneath your bed all day,
you think it was the bent pines
that drove you under here,
or the songs of whales,
too confusing as you held your breath
between the pounding waves.
Or perhaps it was the Indian boy
you accused of stealing,
or your envy of his bright new reel
singing as he cast time after time
into the sea. Or just his words,
"You don't belong here,"
spoken after your father left you on shore
because he fears the sea
arching its back each morning
over the shallow mouth of the Quillayute River.
You cannot forget
that the pines edging the sea
will not straighten for you,
that the boy who hates you now
lives in a gray board shack,
and when you stole a look
through his oiled-paper window,
you saw only shadows,
heard a language more confusing
than whales', and felt
a hunger you could never fill.
Think about changing.
Think about the fog closing in
with its indiscriminate laying on of hands,
or the horn on James Island,
calling to us all, or your mother,
hoarse from shouting your name,
who weeps now that your father returns,
his gunny sack full of salmon.

They love you, and when their voices
turn rough with fear,
break out to say, "No, I'm here!"
And when their blows come,
hold on like those pines,
their roots stronger for such fury,
those pines that even on calm days
bend back in memory of the wind.

HAT ISLAND

When the Cascades lighten
the cove stills.
Low tide drops trawlers
clumsy on their sides,
buoys slack in gravel.
We push our boat to water.
Candlefish swarm just after dawn.

John rakes for bait, and my father
ties #2 Eagleclaws to nylon leader.
I swim with bleeding fish
lanced and bellies up in a bucket.
Enough:
we push beyond the point,
our motor spitting rainbow exhaust
into the Sound.

My father chants for fish.
John sucks air through phantom gills.
From the rocks seals bark songs
that drive fish away.
The tide's eye is open.
John hears fish. Feed rises.
We calculate depth. The bait
flashes in green water.
We prepare with coffee and sweet rolls.

We drift alone.
By counting in sevens
I capture the heart of water.
Taut line feeds my stomach
and I grow scales and pointed teeth.
Cupped in my hand the island
rocks, cabins parading down my thumb.
The crown, needled with pine, sways
above my palm.

I am a giant salmon.
With green fins
I veil the smokey lump of Everett,
slap the banks of Whidbey,
shake sea lice to the Cascades.
Afraid of water the sun hides
behind my head.
I swell and clouds take my shape
drifting . . . the pole
cracks lightning through my hands!

Fish! shouts my father.
No, not now, I whisper,
shriveled beneath my raincoat.
Wait, he says, strip line
as you were taught, wait out each
monotonous wave . . .
There! the strike, the spasms
of fire-red gills again and again.
The pole whips, the reel steams line,
the unseen fish sounds forever.

Now I must fight the waves
with aching arms,
the pole tip up, butt in my stomach.
There is no rhythm,
just the furious tie of green shadow
to black and white boat.
Drop the pole, wind up slowly,
don't shotgun or slack.
He's coming, no more runs,
lead his nose to the net —
with a single heave the salmon lies
boated beating awful time on wood.
He is as big as Hat Island,
until my father stops his dance
with a hammer.

We return at noon
when the tide closes.
John tends the boat. My father
prepares fish for the ritual stove:
guts and gills to crabtraps,
steaks cut and stacked in ice.
Drifting to the point,
I am still fishing.
At my feet a dead seal rots in the sand.
Red holes yawn behind glass eyes,
the nose cut off
for fifty dollars bounty.
As I look in the sand for my father's
steps, crabs mount the feast
and crows settle from the trees
of Hat Island.

FAITH, 1954

The moment I belly flopped
and sank into 12 feet of deep end
I knew that no Red Cross dog
paddle button nor the envious looks
of ten other eight-year-old
non-swimming boys were worth
my aching lungs or even
this green light from above guiding
me down as peacefully as
the street lamps guided me home
each evening from the Seattle YMCA
where I was signed up
and stripped to learn Swimming I.
The first day a black man
in red trunks warned us if we chewed
gum we could choke to death
unless he cut a hole in our throats
to save us. I was so scared
I shivered on the blue tiles folding
gently into the shallow end
where day after day the water blinded
my eyes like hands from behind —
I never guessed whose.
"Save yourself," he yelled,
but I was so skinny my ribs hung me up
like sea anchors. "Paddle, kick,"
he yelled, and I beat my arms numb
to please him and cheated,
my feet kicking off the bottom,
and choked and spat until my hair
went stiff and everything
I owned smelled like Clorox.
"Your day will come," he yelled,
and I imagined myself absolved,
afloat, all paddle, kick, and grace

clear to the far edge
where I would rise from the deep
and stand before the gates of Swimming II.
But on that final day I raised
my hand for wishing, for knowing
what to do but not how,
for every reason save good sense
and the bottom snagging my trunks
and the bubbles escaping my mouth
like self-conscious and embarrassed prayers
rising through the rafters of light
and heard, I knew, I knew,
by my now disgusted savior.

II

He wanted an island all his own: not
necessarily to be alone on it, but to
make a world of his own.

— D. H. Lawrence,
"The Man Who Loved Islands"

CORRESPONDENCE

He finds his place
in Professor Cody's mail-order
rules of punctuation,
licks his pencil as if it needs
to be oiled, and writes, "Dear Jim,"
then nothing for a long time.

Behind him my mother looks up
from her boiling kettle and tells him
to mention clean clothes
and three squares a day. But this
is his letter. He writes,
"Hope your thumb is better,"
knowing it has been for years.

My aim is no better now
than the time he stood over me,
the wood and my thumb hammered,
and he whispered, "Think, think,"
and tapped my forehead to pound
the message home. When I asked
if thinking was like seeing
in the dark, he said nothing.
"The birds have robbed us blind,"
he writes. "The Cascades are clear."

There's too much paper left.
He fidgets in his chair. Maybe
his back aches from these
ten minutes of nonuse or my mother
looks over his shoulder
and he remembers my voice
on the far side of his newspaper,
"Dad, dad . . ." Then her yelling
from the kitchen, "He's talking to you!"

He writes, "$10 enclosed for laundry,"
and licking the pencil one more time,
signs, "Love your father,"
the comma left out on purpose
and the last word started
like a ten penny nail,
with three quick strokes driven home.

LUNCH HOUR AT THE SMITH-WESTERN
NOVELTY COMPANY

In the company of two pigeons
I sit on a tar roof spreading
away from me like land given up on
and burned clean. Beneath me
is where I work, an old hotel turned
speakeasy turned dentist's office
still smelling of cloves,
turned warehouse on this run-down street
in Tacoma, where all the buildings decay
like trees from the inside out.
Over the edge of my coffee cup
a rusty freighter pushes
slowly out to sea. I would sign on
if all else fails but now
I've got to make it here,
not like the man in the story
who moves to smaller and smaller islands,
leaving behind his bickering servants,
his frost-burned orchards,
his silent wife and noisy child.
Here. Well-shorn and well-shod, I say,
giving no credit to my mother
who asks my friends over and over
where she went wrong.
She thinks it's the station wagon
she gave me, the one I drove headlong
down Pacific Avenue, slouched in my seat,
nodding to the girls in the next lane
and piling into a parked car.
Or maybe it's the husband she discarded,
the one she speaks of as a bad choice
and worse idea. She finds
it easy to hate an idea and in my case,
to love one. No kidding, I say.
No kidding.

*   *   *

Early each morning I wind
my way through the streets of Tacoma,
an eye out for the women
who hike their skirts up
in the anonymity of traffic. I push
the company's ancient panel truck
as if it were the English sports car
I will own someday. Then it's four hours
of party hats, paper flowers, the gags
for someone with everything or nothing.
Look: your fortune in a tin box.
Open it and a little boy flops
his penis out and pees on your shoe.

                    *   *   *

The man in the story has left
something out. There's got to be more
than snow piled up against
his stone cottage, the howling gray sea,
and himself huddled around himself
beside a dying stove. Memory, for instance.
How it clings like burrs
caught in the cuff of my new suit.
How all the consequences of choice remain
like my unreadable tattoo.
Even when I try to forget,
I see myself plainer still,
selling encyclopedias door to door,
or pyramids of laundry soap,
or group photographs to families
so poor they believed me when I said
these would be something they could cherish
forever. There's nothing I can do
about my neighbor who laughed
because she babysat me years ago,
who pulled me down to her, her husband
asleep in the next room.
I was so afraid I whispered
she was a fine crystal goblet,
and she shoved me off, knowing I'd lied.

Or the sailor in the bar in Seattle,
who challenged me to pool,
and I lost and lost, made one huge bet,
lost again and ran.
It's as if all I touch touches back
and becomes me. I must learn
all over how to touch.
I could tell the gypsy woman
who shines my shoes
how beautiful she must have been
when she was young. I could search
the eyes of the old news vendor,
three stories down and drunk on a stoop,
for some trace of recognition.

*   *   *

"Up here," I yell, but he doesn't budge.
I throw my half-eaten lunch,
the sack bouncing at his feet, and at once
think how paltry and wrong,
how all that can touch me now
is this harmless man hobbling up the street,
away from a world that falls
around him. I wave my business card,
my name pressed into my fingers,
and throw that too so it flutters
in the wind like a flag cut loose
from a small, ridiculous country.

WITHOUT WARNING

I know now
we are given equal shares
of nothing.
This morning a man
gave back his to the sea.
Far off I swore
I knew him, sure I'd find
his name in all
that's loose and drifting,
all that washed my feet
as I too walked the vague line
between land and sea.
Gulls cried above us.
When he sat down
I thought he was fishing.
But the closer I drew
the farther he seemed,
his arms lifted up,
a red gasoline can tipped
above him, the air
gone ambiguous with fumes.
And when he folded
his hands and nodded
as if he knew that ashes
would never drift,
that horizons lie
four miles off always,
the flames began
like "nothing" shouted
to all of us long at sea,
running to save
something of ourselves,
the brightest light on shore
calling us home.

AN APOLOGY TO A FRIEND
FOR SHOOTING A HOLE IN HIS CEILING

My friend, what have I done
against all learning,
how the pistol's to be held
and where? Eyes dented,
ears stuffed with sound,
I hold your .22 automatic gone
all of a sudden warm.
Stumbling from the kitchen,
you remember just now the gun
you let me see is loaded.
No, I'm alive, thinking
of Mrs. Beeler, my first-grade teacher,
more incensed by my standing mute,
shoulders hunched, palms out,
than by my crime, until today
I hadn't remembered. I confess.
Moments ago I peered down
the bright vertigo of riflings.
My stomach rolled, my legs went loose
as if I leaned too far
over a high staircase railing,
the red blossom I needed
for luck just out of reach, farther,
until that woman's voice,
"James!" and I teetered footloose
frightened by the clear air,
the ground's chamber beneath me
as dark and heavy as lead.
I heard that voice today, turned
the barrel up and stopped thinking.
My friend, the bullet's safe
in your ceiling. My face stings,

the blasted air a woman's hand
striking me in fear,
in anger for all
my dumbstruck, dangerous knowing.
What can I say, my friend,
so frightened now at being alive
all I can do is shrug.

"JUGGLE THE LIMES, GET ONE FREE"

Something's up and you know it.
For weeks I've wandered the aisles,
bought a potato or two, said nothing
even when our hands touched over change.
Now I circle the egg plants
as if what I've lost might be there.

The clock winds down to closing.
If you were to look up now
from stacking apples too high —
one rolls down and you catch it,
your hair bound up, your hands red from washing,
your apron tied twice at the middle —
I'd look down, stuff my pockets with hands,
and whistle.

My fruit stand lady,
I have something important to show you.
I've practiced for weeks, first with scarves
so lazy in the air my hands could find them,
then stones, then china cups and plates,
my hands thinking at last.

Let us place the counter behind us.
Let us focus on the air.
Lock the door, pull down the blinds.
Let me stand before you, all my courage up,
a lime cold and heavy in each hand,
and the third, so like a word between us,
always in the air.

TO THE LADY WHO RENTS CANOES
ON THE TCHFUNCTA RIVER

When I returned your red canoe, its hull
dented out, I told you that the bayou lives.
No news to you I thought, but being young,
northern, in search of something — songs, myself? —
I whispered over the reeds and grass that waved
to me a warning I did not understand.
A cypress led me by its rounded hips,
and through a mouth I glided, breath held still.
Then all was sudden silence watching me,
until an owl, disgruntled, flapped awake,
until the black and dull white cottonmouth
unwound itself and dropped in my canoe.
I paid for the dent, the paddle broken off,
and took with me your slow and practiced words:
"Remember, I told you about the snakes,"
and then, "Y'all come back real soon, you hear?"

THE OLD SWING

Late in this warm June night
I've loaded everything
into the U-Haul except the floor
lamp which lights the corner
I stop sweeping because a bat
glides soundless through the door
and I'm paralyzed, knees shaking,
my broom cocked on my shoulder
as if I'm the last man up, frozen
by stories of heroes crowding
the plate, two out, nobody on,
and one more chance now
the bat curves toward me
like the oldest baseball I remember,
black horsehide loose, spinning,
and I swing my old swing,
foot in the bucket, back creaking
as I screw myself into the rug,
all cracked wrists and knees crossed,
the lampshade driven halfway
across the room that collapses
into darkness, its air gone out
the door with me, silly and frightened,
awed by that perfect pitch,
sure I've found the same old way
to strike out.

THE RECOVERY

At first nobody saw
and the sea and the black sky
couldn't have cared less when the pitch
of a certain wave, a weakness
in the railing, a salmon grabbing
at my hooks launched me
upside down past the gunwale,
"Mary Lou: Westport," the dead exhaust,
and head first into the sea
so quietly only a gull bent back
to wonder.

And what I remembered after the splash
was letting go, forgetting
the broken link, the "what if"
of a minute sooner, a foot this way
or that. All I could do was fall,
keep my mouth shut, and come about
on a new course, straight up, kicking
toward the light.

On deck my father cursed
and my new wife stared
at the progressively wider guides
of a fishing rod rising from the sea,
a noisy reel, a hand, *my* head,
a cigarette butt still clamped in my lips.
And when my father hoisted me on deck
and I felt the rod jerk my hands
and my wife wring out the tail
of my shirt, I knew that somehow
I'd made it like the juggler
who catches his plate
an inch from the floor, or my salmon
whose one last desperate leap
shakes the hook free.

ELEGY FOR AN OLD BOXER

From my window
I watch the roots of a willow
push your house crooked,
women rummage through boxes,
your sons cart away the TV, its cord
trailing like your useless arms.
Only weeks ago we watched the heavyweights,
and between rounds you pummeled the air,
drank whiskey, admonished, "Know your competition!"
You did, Kansas, the '20s
when you measured the town champ
as he danced the same dance over and over:
left foot, right lead, head down,
the move you'd dreamt about for days.
Then right on cue your hay-bale uppercut
compressed his spine. You knew. That was that.
Now your mail piles up, RESIDENT circled
"not here." Your lawn goes to seed. Dandelions
burst in the wind. From my window
I see you flat on your back on some canvas,
above you a wrinkled face, its clippy bow tie
bobbing toward ten. There's someone behind you,
resting easy against the ropes,
a last minute substitute on the card you knew
so well, vaguely familiar, taken for granted,
with a sucker punch you don't remember
ever having seen.

HATCH LAKE, MINNESOTA

Now the wind pushes my boat
toward the rice-stubbled shore,
and I hold my bleeding thumb
beneath the cold of Hatch Lake.
It is August, early morning.
I can smell winter in the air
like a clean shirt frozen on the line.
Far off a loon cries in my ear,
flapping and waddling until the tips
of its wings touch water
once more and it flies
as silently as my blood flows
free of my skin at last.
I have not been spared. Birch trees
lean toward me with notes
explaining all the colors of winter.
The bottom looms up, stained
iron-red by others who have drowned
something of themselves before me,
who must have watched the long-sided fish
sidle exhausted to their boats,
who reached their hands into its jaw
and felt all its weight at once
convulsing, gone, their hands torn
and empty. I have learned
why all talk here honors winter,
that what I leave of myself goes clear
and infinitesimal, washed over and over
on shore where my boat freezes
and rice heads nod like old men
spilling their welcomes
and I step out, delivered by the wind
from all but the pain of healing.

III

LET ME BE RICHARD

My grandmother always tore off
the corner of a two dollar bill
so the bad luck would run out.
I think it spilled on her. Today
she has forgotten my name again.
Before I can say, "No, I'm Jim,"
she tells me my hair has grown back
and my skin is paler than the scars
she shows me, running down her arm
in their perfect memory of boiling water.
It is the only skin on her body
that grows younger with age.
I'm not the priest for whom she mumbles
words from a book that smells
of lilacs, nor her only son,
Richard, who left her to a world as small
and hard as her last silver dollar.
She's lived a long time. I remember
how I once pried two glass stones
from her brooch and hid them
because I mistook the meaning of value.
I've forgotten where. Beneath the elm
that rattles her window? If I can't
find them or turn the handle
of her boiling pot back into the stove,
let me be Richard one day
because I look like him in my silence
and this room is too hot
and she wears three sweaters now
because the edge we have torn from her
has left her empty and cold.

TO FIND A BEAR AT AGNES GORGE

If you find the trailhead
some early spring when snow survives
in daylong shadows,
if you climb alone, stepping
on nothing you can step over,
breathing easy at first,
returning for what you can't remember —
a knit cap, a secret store,
a clue telling you why
the miners left the gorge years ago,
escaping with the thin seam
of their lives —
                    and if you climb
three hard miles that twist
as if water had cut them
from the thick roots of cedars,
sun spilling through, the wind high
above your walking quietly
as if noise were as wrong as fire,
as if you blaze nothing,
as if you give back each breath
you pull in, the grade steeper,
your knapsack timing each step,
your hands pushing your knees
hard around the last bend before Agnes Gorge —
it is then you will see him
watching you.
                    It is then
you will stop, your heart climbing still,
and stare, rewarded for silence,
the bear treed and timid with spring,
a yearling you'll remember later,
unsure of this common ground as you,
who sign all claim away,
you, who own nothing now but good boots,
a way back, and legs fresh as wind.

THE DESERT

The easiest thing to do here is build a road.
    A cow looking for water will,
But more often than not find nothing but itself
    Crazed on jimsonweed, stock-still,
    Sore-bellied, trying to drink up the sand.
And its persistent neighbors — the Swainson's hawk, the crow —
All the harbingers of disaster wait for the end,
    The last cry that shakes the bitterbrush,
        When a few survive
By cleaning the bones of those who travel here and
        End where they arrive.

Yet it is curious how most things adjust:
    The winterfat, the thyme buckwheat
Leaning away from the sand-filled wind, or sagebrush
    Closing down in the midday heat.
And after a meeting of cautious eyes
How the darkling beetle yields to the grasshopper mouse
To the desert night snake to, at last, the burrowing owl —
    This marriage of victim and victor
        With its deadly union
Consummated between the falling sun and the rise
        Of a frozen moon.

Even I may live by turning the earth upside down,
    Piling sand around me for walls.
I wait like a seed underground, then rise each
    Morning to walk the dry rills,
To hunt the black-tailed hare, the sage grouse,
And return before the sun explodes. Some days the air
Will promise rain, and as I watch a few clouds blacken,
    The desert blooms, the sand turning green in
        A moment's shower.
Time to bathe before the sun returns. What blooms
        Will die in an hour.

BINDWEED

There is little I can do
besides stoop to pluck them
one by one from the ground,
their roots all weak links,
this hoard of Lazaruses popping up
at night, not the Heavenly Blue
so like silk handkerchiefs,
nor the Giant White so timid
in the face of the moon,
but poor relations who visit
then stay. They sleep in my garden.
Each morning I evict them.
Each night more arrive, their leaves
small, green shrouds,
reminding me the mother root
waits deep underground
and I dig but will never find her
and her children will inherit
all that I've cleared
when she holds me tighter
and tighter in her arms.

STUMP FARM

for my brother

A crop in perpetual failure
you say, laughing all day beneath a sky
gray as hardpan. We've cut firewood
until my truck groans in its springs,
and now we sit and drink and watch the sky
darken as a bruise darkens, the stumps
gone black on your two muddy acres —
a good idea you thought
until your wife left at night, the wolf
wild in her veins, her headlights
crazy in the trees that fall now
one by one around you. Stump farm —
pasture someday, a good fence,
maybe a single-wide towed in, blocked up,
and water if the pipes don't freeze.

She left what she couldn't move:
the garage you sleep in, your gift horse
that bit her once too often, bruises
rising in her arms like two-petalled flowers,
even your dumb anger no one sees,
that holds the riding crop at your side
when the horse swings backside out,
steel shoes flashing. It's as if
you can't break something inside you
stubborn as stumps that will not budge
come prybar or peavy or weeks of fire,
come desperate late-night seedings of mud
for pasture rising green and even
come spring, come spring.

THE TROUBLE WITH TABLES AND CHAIRS

for Marvin Bell

The trouble is no one's average.
Someone's got to dangle his soles
an inch off the floor or bang his shins
on the table's skirt, that vestige
we no longer hide behind
because our guests attack less frequently
at dinner. Some maker, miter box in hand,
has tried to please us all,
pleasing no one as we search
for one place, angle, set of mind
and seat, scooting and scraping
arm against arm, leg against carpet,
knees crossed and stuck out
of sight and mind so we might lean finally,
elbows propped, into our business.
We teach the odd shapes we own
where clear air is, how to spot
sharp corners and live in small places.
Our elbows and knees grow wise
and silent with memories of their own.
But let us lose ourselves again
to the insurmountable beauty of a woman
or the penetrating questions of a fool,
and our bones forget all they ever knew,
barking themselves crazy at each
corner and edge of every table and chair
until we're out the door, safe
in our shoes, the only furniture that fits
our start down an easy path we know
beneath a wide sky all the way to town.

ICE FISHING

This morning
there is no sun.
Just a weary light seeps
from the clouds.

Asleep the ice groans
as I inch along, tiptoeing
on belief, sliding to my place
alone.

I fear my own weight,
the tenuous clarity,
the horribly familiar face
that squints from darkness,

but I strike
where visions lead me
to fracture the ice with a stone.
The warm mouth opens

as difficult as birth.
My fingers guide me,
tending hooks in the darkness.
I call to what I cannot see.

I give words to what I take:
the perch, still on the ice,
orange and blue, wide-eyed
amazed by the air.

BULL SLAUGHTER

All summer they have praised him
with sugar beets and hay,
given ground where he wanted ground,
water in his concrete trough,
silence and clear, cold mornings
he could fill with bellowing
and his breath drifting
shoulder-high over the fields.
But this morning the woman who fills
his trough stands far away,
hushing her children,
and behind her the man
who brings him sugar beets
kicks at nothing on the ground.
Other men in boots and aprons
watch him so intently that
all of his skin shudders.
They keep the distance he allows them
even now as they clap once
and his knees buckle,
even now as their hands cross
over and over the grinding steel,
even now as they bend down
and bless him with their sharpest knives.

TO THE CATS OF CRETE

Tonight, my second in Crete,
I take my time and watch
the cats leap from the rock walls
silently to their toes, as if cool
etesian wind releases them
after the heat of the day.
I lift my spoon full of sea,
kalamarakia, and rinse my mouth
in *retsina*. If I lived here long enough,
they would be delicious,
my pants would go baggy,
I would sleep in the afternoon
and rise each evening, enough
drachmas in my pocket to eat again,
the waiter who slaps my table
with his towel able to pronounce my name.

I eat slowly, the oil, rich and yellow,
soaking my bread. Finished, I lean back
and drink to the cats of Crete,
scenting the legs of my table,
circling me just out of reach,
more silent in their watching
than wind tonight through the tamarisk.

To long hind legs and knotted tails!
To patient, unblinking eyes!
To *ouzo* warm in my mouth, dimmed lights,
the waiter leaning on his broom,
and then I rise, a few drachmas
pinned beneath my glass,
a tentacle of squid left on my plate
in tribute to the cats
that have always lived here,
that will sing to me again,

xénos, both stranger and guest,
who has learned how to sleep here at last
with the window open and the wind
filling the room all night
with a newborn's crying.

MOUNTAIN PASS

How we sought safety, but loved danger.

— Louise Bogan

Hours in low gear, I have climbed
south from Ciudad Victoria,
away from the boy who hawks
lizards beside the road,
the old women who wait for the bus
that slaughters a man's pigs
because he herds them
into the wrong journey.
I have left money for the ground
I slept on, passed the last *Alto* sign,
where a young *federal* threaded
his hands deep into my suitcase,
found nothing I needed
and waved me back onto this road
that twists down in my mirrors
like a hair shaken loose
onto the skirt of the ragged mother,
Sierra Madre, who rocks me
back and forth until safe.
I find, one level moment above it all,
a horse dead on the shoulder —
its final master as startled as I —
stepping into its wings
and gliding as easy as the air rising
from all I've left behind
gone over my shoulder
before the sign *Curva Peligrosa*
wakes me, its words so lovely
my ears pop and I shift,
clutch the map promising so much ahead,
and brake hard, hard.

LEARNING HOW TO BUY FISH

Outside the *pescadería*
we sit on an old bench
and the ragged pigeons,
having dodged so much flying tortilla,
walk between our legs
and we still can't hit them.
I am not so foolish, you think,
as Tony, the insurance salesman from Mazatlan,
who wants to marry your daughter
but takes "no" for an answer.
Though not so smart yet
to tell the old fish from the new
hidden deep in the bloodstained ice.
I count well enough
but make weak accusations.
I fail to offer nothing for something.
I mind too much
the boy who pulls the stalest carp
tail first from the ice
and flags his mouth with a red hand
and sniggers. Or the woman
behind the scales, tucking a strand
back into her hair so tight
it pulls the color from her face.
She tells us we have no idea
what fish cost, that we would steal
food from her children's mouths.
I believe her. You rap my shin
with your cane, tell me
we will sit here as long as it takes —
though your wife is waiting
and her soup's undone —
as long as it takes to teach
one pigeon not to peck
at everything thrown his way.

BUS RIDE,
PIE DE LA CUESTA

The air is hot noise.
I bounce on the back wheel
as the driver of our bus
churns its heart with the shift.
Beside me an old man smokes,
his gasoline cans stopped with rags,
jiggling on the floor.
I stare out the window and
try not to imagine. Beside the road
a young woman walks straight up
beneath the water she carries home.
Her legs are saplings
and I see at her hips the wind turn
the leaves over and over.
Even when she spits on the road,
I think she is beautiful.
I want her to notice me, to rinse
my hands that ache from holding on,
but she will not,
not with her eyes set for balance,
not for me at the edge of sight,
another face in the window,
a rumble, a fume passing on.

IV

IZANAGI AND IZANAMI

19th century Japanese

In this picture
two Shinto gods summon
a sea of white-crested applause
for this their creation of Japan.
It was no easy work
to fashion stone and sea
from the draft of their souls,
yet his blows rang the mountains up
and her hands turned down
a bed of meadows.

Their work is nearly finished.
Clouds mat the home
upon which she gazes.
For the final touch
he, deft with a lance,
carves their names
as the boughs of cherry trees,
the leaves the faces of children.

MISTAKEN IDENTITY

Tonight because the rain softens
all my mistakes, streaking the window,
and because the only person I know
in this town is Jean, the waitress
who logs on her pad my litany
of hunger, I think it's you

I see out the corner of my eye,
crossing against the light, your hair
tucked safe beneath your collar.
You still walk head down and hurried.
You've lost yourself again
to the phone or radio, its sad clarinet

sounding like your father's
those Sundays in Rosalia, those Sundays
we wandered the back way home
through cut fields, past headstones
overgrown with flowers
we promised to name later.

Here: knotweed and meadowrue.
I want to tell you we held ourselves
so close we never saw this town,
the rain falling all at once
on a dark street where you see
in the glance that strangers allow

no one you have ever known,
or this: me, coatless and mistaken,
stepping from the shadows,
a man who knew it could never be,
a man who stares at the suddenly clear sky
and finds the stars are missing.

RENTED ROOM

When the lovers upstairs
find themselves
on their worn, rented carpet,
it isn't the noise I mind,
rattling the dust
from my pale, bloomless violet,
nor their names whispered
through the ceiling
as if announced from some flat
white heaven. For them
I turn my pockets out
and two coins wheel
after themselves under the couch.
Then I search at once
for anything I've forgotten —
pacing the floor, stacking
books, poring over
letters so old all I remember
is the smell of paper.
Nothing seems to help.
Tonight condemns me
to hold these lovers
as gently as leaves hold dust.
And it isn't the strength
I need to love them
as a printer loves his paper
for the edge it gives
someone else's words,
nor the silence that falls
now they have finished.
No, it's more the fear I mind
that they might find me
standing on a chair,
hands pressed to the ceiling
to lift them as if
loneliness were a bed to lie on
and reason enough
to begin again.

MOVING

The house is sold.
All that's left of yours is one old dresser
stored in the basement, the back facing out.
You told me it was given by friends,
and your wife soaked the wood with oil, darkened
the scratches with walnut meat,
lined the drawers with paper and petals and clothes
that smelled each morning of linseed and roses.

          You cannot lift
this dresser by yourself. I am here for no wages
but talk and maybe a few beers
to dull my skinned knuckles, which will heal.
I give you my knuckles.
You open and close, open and
close the drawers. No rubbing will erase
the long burn of a cigarette left
out of anger or love,
nor all the nicks and dents, the language
of a small, lost civilization
you translate one more time with your hands. Come on.

The floor creaks.
Someone who lives here is waiting.
A child cries in the attic,
and you scan the joists in the old reflex of concern.
You say, "Let's get on with it,"
and I give you my back
to help lift this weight, the clumsy silence,
the dresser you hug for the last time
slowly up the stairs.

WHEN THE FOGGERS COME

I come to her the same way as always
through the dry culvert,
past the windbreak poplars
where starlings roost
as noisy as bad axles turning
nowhere but into the night.
I see her through her window,
wishing for the cold season,
the chilblains reddening her cheeks
like a fever. And when I step inside,
my hands full of primroses,
she tells me she cannot decide whether
to tie her hair back for the heat
or let it fall like a folding screen
so no one can see.

I ask for her old stories:
how her grandfather speaks
from his Bible, its broken spine,
his cramped marginal notes
bringing that old man back
to press her to a window
as her father drops slaughtered chickens
onto the hip-deep snow of Ohio.
How she once believed their blood turned black
because the sun stole the red,
spreading it thin and clear behind the trees
from one end of the sky to the other.

And when I tell her there's something
certain in the telling of this
like a story before bed,
she tells me the sun steals even her windows
black and the mutter of engines we hear
is the foggers come
for mosquitoes that once traded
her blood for sleep.

And when I hold her, my arms like bedclothes,
the smell of kerosene seeping
beneath the door,
she shivers, knees up,
waiting for her own warmth to fill my arms,
the warmth in which she remembers
she feared no sleep.

TOO EARLY SATURDAY MORNING

the woman next door whacks
a stick on my fence, shouting.
I shake the sleep out
of my ears. I don't understand.
She's ignored me from the start,
hung her wash or picked fruit
while I tidied my two new acres.
Now she yells, "Your goat, your goat!"
and watches me run barefoot,
never mind tackweed or thorns,
past chickens digging
in my garden, past her startled horse,
to the still dark pen where
Mathilda lies, her neck bleeding,
and Thunder, my year-old shepherd,
has learned how to begin
but not yet how to finish
murder. I show him: one hand fast
behind his ear lifts him, legs
dangling, slams him
back down to earth, growling.
The too easy tightening of my hands,
thumbs buried in his neck,
and at once each of us sees
how such things are done.
He cries. I let go, simply afraid,
and the woman next door,
the woman who has lived there all
her life, looks on,
one foot poised on my fence,
ready to cross over.

SUMMER STORM

Even loving seems too much
on this hot day. In the late afternoon
we swell with the accumulation
of small matters like so many
slips of paper on which we've written
notes to ourselves.
I rest my hand where your neck slopes
to your shoulder. You know I always do this.
You say my hand is heavy.
You ask if it is raining and will I see?
Out there the color bleeds
from our board fence, the trunks of maples,
their heat-soaked leaves. Now lightning so far
away we hear no thunder.
Then rain, as if you called up the steam
from our road in greeting,
called up the small wind that lifts the leaves,
their undersides as pale as the skin
behind your wrist.
                    You touch my shirt.
I tell you I was a young boy once
caught in the rain, hiding
between stacks of split wood where the grass
lay white and dying. I held
tarpaper over my head and listened
to the rain's noise. Then drunk
one time I slept in someone's half-built house,
out of the rain, curled up with plaster,
afraid of the crawl space and
alone. You tell me
you will listen if I have more to say.
You wrap yourself in a sheet,
one side open. The steam rising. Listen.
There is always more to say.

ACORNS

Outside the wind picks up.
Oak trees, their skirts blown,
drop acorns on the house

next door. It is dark.
We are new to this town.
I mistake the clatter

for buckshot or boys pitching
rocks as I used to.
On the floor you cut and sew

muslin, drapes for the window
I stand at, thinking of old towns,
a single bulb burning

in a window five states away.
Another shot! Behind me
another stitch sewn.

SOLSTICE

1. *Summer*

Sometimes thought dries up
like the stream beside my house
in the dead of summer
when the bed stones remember
what it was to expand.
Take, for instance, my rattling ice
in a glass and drawing
one cube across my forehead
and throwing it — a lazy
sidearm into this day full of heat,
full of my neighbor's clapping
her slippers to wake all dust,
full of hummingbirds
rifling her trumpet flowers,
full of sparrows beneath my feeder,
bathing in the soft dirt
at the far side of my yard
where the ice in its perfectly
dying arc lames one
in the wing. I couldn't have
hit it if I'd tried
or felt anything like I feel now,
walking barelegged in thorns
where the sparrow has lost itself,
where I find nothing to heal
but something bedded
in a hard place, beneath thought,
perfection its final aim.

2. *Winter*

This morning the moon
sets so close the tallest branch
of my crab apple tree passes
behind it. Out my window
I see my neighbor late again,
hurrying in the dark
to fill his arms with firewood.
The robins, at work already,
clip the crab apples from my tree.
I think it measures only itself
all year: red blossoms dropping
no farther than the reach
of its farthest branch, then leaves,
now crab apples lost in the snow.
I have waited another year
for the sun to rise
no farther south than ever.
I have waited for the beauty
and sadness of this like a child
who backs into his father's door,
one hand flat on his head,
knowing he has grown no taller,
or the robins that leave
in their search the bare snow outline
of the branches of my tree,
or my neighbor who drives to work at last,
one of his taillights out,
one bright like a small, bitter apple
found in the snow.

FATHER-IN-LAW, SIX YEARS LATER

He edges into the room
he has given us, cold this morning,
and perhaps sees his daughter
not as she is,
her arm over me,
light passing through the curtains
onto the foot of our bed,
but as she was looking up at him
in the snapshot framed on his dresser
behind his billfold and keys.

He stops.
Or in my half-sleep I stop him
as if we meet again
for the first time. Does he offer
the same chair like unsettled country
for me to fidget in
before a tribunal of aunts, before candles,
before the rites of supper
and the mysterious fumbling of knives
and spoons? I am neither
what he hoped for nor condemned.

Beside our suitcase
burst on the floor, our clothes pell-mell
on a chair, he waits for his daughter
to look up at him as before.
As slowly as the years lie down
he wades through the light
to give her away again, one hand on her shoulder,
and with the other he wakes me,
wakes us all.

LOST IN AMSTERDAM

Late in the day I left you
sleeping in the last room in town,
descended the stairs
through the landlord's butcher shop,
and returned hours later,
haggard by lines, our bags found,
our tickets to somewhere
crumpled in my pocket.
At the corner I bought you flowers,
rosebuds not far from bloom,
from an old man who must have heard you crying,
awake too soon from hard sleep.
Maybe you descended the stairs
into a strange city, the wind gone cold,
and found even your language lost
on the butcher who grimaced,
wiping his hands on a red-stained towel,
or his wife who cradled
your arm and waved at the thin street
as if calling her children home.
If you found nothing more
than black water running
through an abandoned canal
and all bridges away from here empty,
then maybe you climbed those stairs again
and lay down to listen:
a woman's sweeping outside your door,
the butcher scraping his block,
the calling of an old man
who charged me far too little
for the roses he pressed in my hand,
so I might lay them beside us,
so we might leave them tomorrow
blooming in a borrowed vase
on a clean and polished table.

CANOE CROSSING

I should have known.
In late August the wind shows up.
Priest Lake contracts,
full of itself, its white caps hissing
like breath through my teeth.
Nearly home, I should have known
you'd turn from the bow
to right our daughter, her fat red jacket
holding her in sleep.
                              And though we drift
and waves slap us clumsy,
we spill only into what might happen.
Fear scolds you into the wind,
drops me to my knees,
pushes all my weight into my arms over
and over until my back talks
in a language so bare no matter
how wide I open my mouth
I can tell you nothing of what
my muscles say.
                              I'd give anything
to deliver us to one still room,
its table and chairs, a lamp trimmed and lit
in the window of our cabin
raised between the damp trees
like a wooden crown on the beach's white head —
anything to rest cock-eyed and grounded,
the hull stone-scraped,
my arms too dead to lift our daughter
clear of this wet, aluminum belly
where she cries out
for the body's mother tongue
drowned at last in the cold air of waking.

COMPOSING TWO BLACK AND WHITE PHOTOGRAPHS

1.

Something said or not said
and we drop into silence.
Kneeling on an empty dock,
you stop down black blacker at the edge
of my shadow cutting the white
of this whitest stucco wall.
I am seated on gray two by fours.
On my left the boarded window
of a bait house. On my right a gasoline pump,
locked, filling itself.
You have told me to look at anything
but you squeezing yourself
into the red inch-space of your lens.
O.K. I watch the oak trees
behind you, kibitzing, all their bets
lost to the winning season.
You look for balance:
my elbows propped on my knees,
my hands cupped around my face
like blinders, my reflection wobbling
in the water between us.
It is a bright, cold day.
You have left me to focus
the shadows above my head, wavering
black, white, black, white —
left me until late in a darkened room
in the yellow light that exposes nothing.
You work on detail: equal time
for the window, me, the stucco wall.
More time, more light
for the gasoline pump, "burned" you say,
until its numbers sharpen up
to zeroes.

2.

A frozen pipe, a valve rusted shut,
the concrete walls of a bait tank
filled with rainwater. What draws you
is the reflection of an oak tree
sealed shut for the winter,
how it grows out of a concrete wall
toward you as if your lens
shines brighter than the sun.
I would sooner replace this cold day
with the owl we baited last summer,
gliding down from the tree
two hands' full of belly first
into the cups of its wings.
Ten feet away we sat dead still
and the owl, wings fanning the dock,
watched the distance between us.
Remember? The tree is empty.
I would hold you now
out of this clear, cold wind,
out of the too short days that seal
the ends of everything,
hold you until the barred owl returns
to drive its talon once more
into a minnow's eye. No. You wander
into yourself, focus behind
the walls until the water turns white
and a few black leaves drift back
to their branches. This is the picture,
and somewhere cropped out,
hands in my pockets,
I do the difficult thing for love's sake:
I let you go.

SPIDER

Tarantula or wolf spider —
I can't tell kneeling in the dim light,
our walkway shadowed but still warm.
Maybe she draws heat from the stones.
Maybe she dreams of lost burrows
quilted in silk. And why I'm kneeling
here, I don't know. Maybe to rest,
maybe to live alone and wonder
how this spider calls up my past
where bitten once I sleep in fear
of invisible webs at night.
Or simply to imagine myself,
my thorax as fat as dumplings,
my eyes swiveling all directions
at once, leg tip to hairy leg tip
as wide as my hand that leads her
lightly out of harm, startled.
I stand, awake, full of the news
and ring the bell to find my wife
and daughter, who must know already,
hand in hand, healing the day by dancing.

HEADLONG

Why is it now,
as I near forty and my child
runs headlong on her legs,
that I remember Larry McMurray's '59
Ford station wagon I bought
one morning and wrecked that night,
the hood standing straight up
and as far back as the gas cap
a moonscape of dents and sprung doors?
My first full stop announced
with a bang, a glass-littered street,
and hours of sirens dying
all the way to Tacoma General.
Where was I going
eight times past Frisco Freeze?
I remember the rearview mirror gone,
and high on the windshield,
like a print in drypoint,
the faint likeness of my hair.
Sixteen, in love with wreckage,
I thought I'd never die,
right for once in a world as wrong
as the drunk who hit me,
his wife unconscious and bleeding
onto his lap. Wake up.
What am I thinking?
Will I tell my daughter this
when she outruns her legs?
Or that I drive to her each night
miles beneath the limit,
my vision gone, my hands tight
on the wheel all the way home
where I lock the door,
bandage her skinned knee,
tell her a story she doesn't believe:
how I once flew down streets
too fast, lucky as a backseat dog asleep,
and reckless all the wrong ways.

ACKNOWLEDGMENTS

Grateful acknowledgment is made to the editors of the following magazines in which some of these poems first appeared.

THE AGNI REVIEW: "Rowing for Water"

ATLANTIC MONTHLY: "Bull Slaughter," "Mountain Pass," "An Apology to a Friend for Shooting a Hole in His Ceiling"

THE CALIFORNIA QUARTERLY: "Solstice"

CIMARRON REVIEW: "To the Cats of Crete," Part 2 of "Composing Two Black and White Phtographs" under the title "Composing a Black and White Photograph, Lake MacBride, Iowa"

THE GREENFIELD REVIEW: "Ice Fishing"

IRONWOOD: "Hatch Lake, Minnesota"

THE IOWA REVIEW: "Correspondence"

THE MISSOURI REVIEW: "After Listening to Jack Teagarden . . ."

NORTHWEST REVIEW: "Green Lake"

POETRY: "Bus Ride, Pie de la Cuesta," "Lost in Amsterdam," "Headlong," "Stump Farm"

POETRY NORTHWEST: "Bindweed," "The Gift," "Rented Room"

PRAIRIE SCHOONER: "Elegy for an Old Boxer"

QUARTERLY WEST: "The Desert"

THE SLACKWATER REVIEW: "Hat Island"

SNAPDRAGON: "Izanagi and Izanami"

The quotation that begins Part II is from THE WOMAN WHO RODE AWAY AND OTHER STORIES, by D. H. Lawrence. Copyright 1928 by D. H. Lawrence and renewed in 1956 by Frieda Lawrence Ravagli. Reprinted by permission of Alfred A. Knopf, Inc.

Headlong was composed in Intertype Baskerville
with handset Baskerville Foundry display type
by Donald M. Henriksen, Scholarly Typography, Salt Lake City.